HONDURAS AND GUATEMALA.

To the Editors of the National Intelligencer:

In the *Intelligencer* of the 16th inst., you have allowed "a retired citizen," under the pretence of "vindicating the cause of truth," to malign a respectable Association of American citizens, and to falsify and misrepresent the "facts of history," in all that concerns the existing relations between the States of Honduras and Guatemala in Central America. The Association thus vilified have a right to ask, and the cause of truth requires, at your hands, a vindication as ample as the outrage of which you have been made the medium is gross and unjustifiable.

The assassin strikes in the dark, and the slanderer and falsifier usually chooses an anonymous disguise under which to make his assaults, and evade the responsibility which attaches to his conduct. This is precisely the course pursued by your correspondent, "the retired citizen." It needs no gift of divination to discover his animus or penetrate his motives, both of which are as base as his anonymous exhibition of them is cowardly.

So far as he assumes to state the origin of the present differences between Honduras and Guatemala, and to indicate the political position and tendencies of these States respectively, he is guilty not only of gross misrepresentation but of deliberate falsehood.

Whatever may be the conflict of claims between these two States, in respect of boundaries, that diversity has had little or no connection with the present differences, which are directly due to the invasion of the acknowledged and indisputable territories of Honduras by armed forces from Guatemala. This your "retired" correspondent does not pretend to deny; but he seeks to justify the act, by the assertion that "certain lawless marauders, recruited and armed in Honduras, made hostile inroads into Guatemala," and that when repulsed they "invariably sought and found shelter in Honduras."

Now all this is mere assertion, unsustained by proof, and withal, false in fact. That citizens of Guatemala, driven out by the bloody and unsparing hand of the Indian Dictator of that wretched State, have sought refuge in Honduras, as well as in the States of Chiapas and San Salvador, is undoubtedly true. Such has been the political condition of Central America, as in fact of all Spanish America, for many years, that there is hardly a person of any distinction, political or social, who has not been oftener than once a refugee. And because a man is a refugee in those countries, it no ways follows that he is a criminal. It may be true that some of the political refugees of Guatemala, in Honduras, abused the asylum granted them, and sought to incite opposition in the former State against the parties in power who expelled them. But whoever asserts that the Government of Honduras was in any way a party to such efforts, asserts an untruth, and slanders the really liberal and high-minded men at the head of affairs in that State. They have not only discountenanced all such efforts, but have actively interfered to prevent them. If their interference has not always been effective, it is not surprising, considering the difficulties of communication and the wild nature of the country, which offers ample opportunities of concealment for the evil-disposed. Even the United States, with all its resources, has not always been able to prevent bodies of men from leaving its territories with hostile intent on its neighbors.

With a full and clear knowledge of these facts, I assert, and shall prove, that Honduras actively interfered to prevent any disturbance of Guatemala by persons within its borders; and that the invasion by Guatemala was a wanton act of aggression, attended by the most horrible outrages, not upon political refugees, but on the quiet and unoffending citizens of Honduras, old men, women, and children, entirely unconnected with political affairs.

On the 18th of June, 1852, the town of Zacapa, in Guatemala, was assaulted by a small body of armed men. By some, they were supposed to be from San Salvador; by others, from Honduras; others still supposed them to be—as they probably were—one of the systematic bands of robbers which, in Guatemala alone, of all the States of Central America, infest the public roads, and, as in Mexico, make a trade of robbery. As soon as the information of this act reached Gracias, the frontier department of Honduras, the Commandant of that department despatched the following letter to the Government at Comayagua:—

SANTA ROSA, July 15th, 1852.

To the Minister of War:

SIR: I have received information of the movement of insurrectionists of Guatemala on the frontier, near Copan, and have, in consequence, proceeded to raise an additional force of 50 men, so as to be in readiness, the instant I shall receive authority from the Government, to proceed to put them in check. I have also sent Gen. Toro with a detachment to watch the reported proceedings near Playon. Although I have no direct orders for the contingency, I cannot permit the towns of the frontier to suffer in consequence of the acts of these lawless men; and in case I learn of the appearance of any of the insurrectionists, (*facciosos,*) I shall proceed to disarm them, and to reduce them if they resist.

Signed: JOSE DE ZELAYA.

It will be well to remember the name of this officer, for he is precisely the man who was subsequently robbed by Gen. Grenados in Santa Rosa, and for whose robbery the "retired citizen" is an apologist.

The answer of the Minister of War to Gen. Zelaya was dated "Comayagua, July 27th, 1852," and is conceived in the same spirit of opposition to the disturbers of the public peace. It says: "*The Government approves of the steps which you have taken to repress the facciosos, for it can never permit the territory of Honduras to become an asylum for them wherein to carry on their aggressions against other States.*"

It then proceeds to instruct Gen. Zelaya to arrest such persons as he may find in arms or concerned in illegal enterprises upon Guatemala, be they Guatemalans or citizens, and confine them for trial. It, however, warns him not to allow his zeal "to carry him beyond the boundary, in order to avoid all ground of complaint on the part of Guatemala."

In consequence, Gen. Zelaya proceeded to the frontier, and captured all persons known or suspected to be concerned in disturbing the peace of Guatemala, at the same time confiscating whatever arms and munitions of war the *facciosos* had collected. Another officer, Col. Pineda, was equally active. These measures were commended in the official paper of Guatemala of Sept. 11, 1852, "*as evidences that the Government of Honduras was animated by the best of feelings, and had acted with justice and rectitude.*"

The exertions of the authorities of Honduras were continued until all symptoms of disorder were repressed, when the extraordinary forces, except some small parties of observation, were dismissed. It was then that disturbances broke out in the town of Gualan, in Guatemala. They were precisely of the kind which occur monthly, in one part or another of that anarchical dictatorship, and it was never pretended that they originated in Honduras. But, under the pretence of pursuing the disaffected, Solares, the Commandant of Chiquimula in Guatemala, at the head of 500 men, not only passed the boundary of Honduras, but penetrated to the town of Copan. This invasion took place in the latter part of October, less than a month after the Government of Guatemala had officially returned its thanks to that of Honduras for its "prompt and efficacious suppression of the *facciosos.*" Had the invasion by Solares, indefensible on any ground, been limited solely to passing the borders, it is not likely the act would have led to difficulties.

But his path was marked by rapine and slaughter. Haciendas were robbed, women violated, and a number of inoffending citizens wantonly shot. The little corps of observation at Copan was attacked and driven out. In short, language is inadequate to characterize in deserved terms the atrocities committed by the invaders. No band of savages could have behaved with greater cruelty and barbarity.

It will not do for any apologist for Guatemala to deny these statements; it is a task which the Government of that so-called Republic has never undertaken; for the proof, horrible and disgusting as are its details, is at hand!

Of course this violence sent a thrill of horror and indignation throughout Honduras, and roused the deepest excitement. The Government addressed an earnest and firm note to that of Guatemala, recounting the facts, and asking that the invasion be disavowed, the officer concerned in it reprimanded, and the damages repaired. This letter was written January 2d, 1853. Meantime, reports reaching the capitol of other meditated violations of the territory of the State, Gen. Cabañas, the President, hastened to the frontier, with a small body of men; and an extraordinary session of the Congress of the State was convened to meet at Intibucat, near Gracias. The sole response to the complaints of Honduras was a curt and offensive note from the Government of Guatemala, charging the authorities of Gracias, who had so effectively put down the *facciosos,* with a privity to their designs, and concurrence in them! This unfounded charge was indignantly repelled, and satisfaction again demanded by Honduras.

The correspondence on both sides now became excited, and Carrera, Dictator of Guatemala, also raised troops, and stationed himself near the frontier. The Legislature of Honduras met in April. Its members were greatly irritated by the conduct of Guatemala, and it required all the moderation and influence of Gen. Cabañas to prevent an open declaration of war.

This state of things continued until, after some hesitation on the part of Guatemala, the preliminaries to an understanding were made by the appointment of Commissioners on both sides, who met in Esquipulas, and on the 19th of April, signed a Convention. This Convention provided,

1. That Guatemala should indemnify the sufferers by the invasion at Copan and Casapa.

2. That Guatemala should liberate all the citizens of Honduras which it had carried off from the above-named places.

3. Each party should hereafter respect the territory of the other, and that under all circumstances, all difficulties should be regulated by friendly means.

4. That to place the relations of the two States on the best footing, the parties should, as soon as possible, proceed to negotiate a treaty of friendship, commerce, and boundaries.

5. Honduras should concentrate all refugees from Guatemala, until the terms on which they should be permitted to return to their homes should be fixed by treaty.

6. The Convention to be ratified within six days.

Now mark the utter falsehood and dishonesty of your "retired citizen!" *This treaty was ratified immediately* (on the 23d) *by the Government of Honduras, while that of Guatemala refused its ratification!* Your disingenuous correspondent would make it appear that the failure of the Convention was due to the conduct of Honduras! And yet he has the audacity to set himself up as a "vindicator of truth," and a teacher of morals.

By this action of Guatemala, in repudiating the work of its own Commissioners, the misunderstanding between the States became more complicated and asperous. The Legislature adjourned after empowering the Executive to declare war, in case all efforts to obtain reparation should fail. Finally, Gen. Cabañas, wearied out with evasions and delays, in the month of July advanced upon Guatemala. The policy of this extreme step may be doubted, but the character of the outrage on Honduras, and the bad faith of Guatemala, were ample justification for the reprisal. He soon reduced the department of Chiquimula, occupying successively the towns of Esquipulas, Chiquimula, and Zacapa, but everywhere conducting with moderation, permitting not the slightest excesses on the part of his troops, and scrupulously paying for whatever necessaries he required. This honorable conduct, it may be remarked, is characteristic of Gen. Cabañas, whose hands alone, of all the leaders which Central America has produced, are unstained with blood, and upon whose whole conduct, during more than twenty years of public life, there does not rest a single stain! In all these respects, he is in decided contrast to the Indian Carrera, whom a handful of monarchists and bigots in Guatemala have carried into power, through a series of murders and assassinations, unparalleled in number and atrocity by any thing this continent, and all the years of anarchy in Spanish America, have ever witnessed!

Your anonymous correspondent, in his zeal to misrepresent Honduras, cannot announce this advance of Gen. Cabañas without violating truth. He says: "In July, Gen. Cabañas, at the head of an army of malcontents and renegades, *again* invaded Guatemala." The attempt is here made to convey the falsehood that the invasion of Copan by Solares was in retaliation for a previous invasion of Guatemala by Gen. Cabañas! In this wise, your "retired citizen" vindicates "the truth of history!"

The entrance into Chiquimula was undertaken by Gen. Cabaña with a very inadequate force; and upon the advance of large reinforcements from Guatemala, and in consequence of disaffection among his own troops, he was obliged, after some skirmishing, to fall back upon Gracias, which he did, slowly, and without precipitation. He was followed by the forces of Guatemala to Santa Rosa, when he retired to San José, where he made a final stand. The Guatemalan force, under a Gen. Garcia Grenados, entered Santa Rosa on the 19th of July. They found the town entirely deserted, for the inhabitants knew too well the brutal character of the invaders of Copan, to trust their own lives, or the honor of their wives and daughters, in their power. The sequel proved the wisdom of their conduct; for no sooner had the Guatemalan troops entered the town, than they commenced an indiscriminate pillage, in which officers and men emulated each other in deeds of robbery and wanton destruction.

It so happens that I was at Santa Rosa, both before and after the occupation by the troops of Guatemala, and am perfectly well informed of all that took place. With this knowledge, I pronounce the entire statement of your anonymous correspondent, in relation to that event, as wholly and maliciously false. It is utterly impossible that any assurance of "protection" from the Guatemalan General could have reached the town without my knowledge. But even if it had, there is not a man in Central America who would have trusted to it. The people there know too well how much faith to place in the savage hordes of Carrera, and his equally unscrupulous subordinates!

The notorious, wholesale sack of Santa Rosa, is disposed of by your correspondent as "some trifling disorders" committed by the soldiers, in consequence of finding the town "without inhabitants and provisions!" And the general robbery of all property which could be carried off, and the wanton destruction of that which it was not possible to remove, is resolved by the same "vindicator of truth" into the seizure of the goods of "a well-known instigator of the invasion!"

These goods were the property of Gen. José de Zelaya, whom we have already had occasion to notice for his prompt and efficacious action in preventing the refugees and *facciosos* of Guatemala from making the territories of Honduras the theatre of their operations upon their own State! These goods, valued at upwards of $40,000, were the property of the same Gen. Zelaya who had been lauded by name, but a short time previously, by the Government of Guatemala, for his "honorable rectitude" in preserving the neutrality of Honduras, and suppressing disorders on the frontiers!

But the "seizures," as your correspondent amiably characterizes the Guatemalan robberies, were not confined to the property of Gen. Zelaya. There was not a store, shop, or dwelling in the whole town of Santa Rosa, which escaped plunder. As I have said, all property which could not be carried off, was destroyed. The mirrors and lamps in the houses were broken; fires were made of the sofas, beds, and other furniture; and the tobacco, the principal product of the vicinity, was burnt in the streets! Even the churches did not escape, but were equally violated, and their more valuable ornaments carried off. Cattle were slaughtered in the salas of the best houses, and their entrails left to putrefy there, and in the courts. The records of the municipality were destroyed, and the public buildings defaced. In short, no act of destruction which an unrestrained and savage soldiery could devise, was omitted. For three days this barbarous saturnalia was continued, when the invaders, fearing the general uprising and summary revenge of the people of the department, retreated precipitately across the frontier, leaving their path marked with fire and blood. Such were the "trifling disorders" of your veracious correspondent!

But the robberies of the Guatemalan General were not limited to the property of the natives. The property of foreigners met no greater respect. A valuable assortment of silks and merinoes, belonging to a French merchant residing in the place, was appropriated by the chivalrous General Grenados, and his principal officers. The French flag, which sheltered them, was torn down, and trampled under foot. And in the subsequent correspondence which took place between the French Consul-General and the Government of Guatemala on the subject, the former very justly characterized the whole conduct of Grenados and his soldiers as that of "*ladrones*, disgraceful to the nineteenth century!"

I now come to the affair of Omoa. The fort of Omoa surrendered to Colonel Zavala, in command of a Guatemalan force, in deference to the wishes of the principal merchants of the place, who sought to avert a conflict, on the 24th of August, 1853. The first article of the capitulation is as follows:

Art. 1. The commander of the fort, considering the small force at his command, the state of the fort, and in deference to the wishes of the municipality and foreign agents, agrees to evacuate the fort at one o'clock this day, with the garrison, arms, and park of artillery, ("*guarnacion y tren de fusilerea parque.*") But in order that no labor may be uselessly expended in taking out things which will require to be reïntroduced hereafter, said arms, &c., ("*tren de fusilerea,*" &c.,) may remain as a deposit in the hands of the U. S. Consul.

Art. 2 contained a stipulation that, in consideration of this step, the Guatemalan commander should reëmbark his troops and evacuate the place "within three days."

This convention or capitulation was accepted by Capt. Medina, commander of the fort, on the following express condition appended to the document, viz.:

"*With the express condition that the Port shall be evacuated by the troops of Guatemala within four days, and that they shall not touch any piece of artillery nor any other article left in the fort.*"

Yet, in violation of these stipulations, the Guatemalans commenced carrying off the armament of the fort, and had embarked five heavy brass guns and two mortars, when further proceedings were stopped by the earnest remonstrance of the American Consul, in whose care the armament had been placed by the capitulation.

Yet your mendacious correspondent says that the Guatemalans violated no faith at Omoa, and that the charge that they did so "is as malicious as it is groundless!" Most rare "vindicator of the truth of history!"

In order to completely stultify himself, it only remains for your correspondent to turn apologist for British aggressions in Central America. This is an appropriate and fitting work for the eulogist of the assassin Carrera, and the vilifier of the liberal and republican State of Honduras! He is welcome to all the honors he can earn in such a congenial undertaking. But he cannot deny that the vessels engaged in the attack on Omoa, in part at least, were under the British flag, and furnished from the establishment of Belize. The official evidence exists in the Department of State. Nor can he deny that recently a large quantity of incendiary documents from Guatemala, addressed for distribution to the British Consul in Honduras, were intercepted by the Government of the latter State. Your correspondent's blunders in dates, and his statements as concerns the seizure of Roatan, etc., may be passed over as simple specimens of irredeemable ignorance, not remarkably becoming in a "vindicator of the truth of history."

It is also appropriate in your correspondent to insult and belie the Liberal party of Central America, while he exalts the aristocratic oligarchy to which they are opposed. In this task he will find himself in entire opposition to every observer of repute who has written on the political condition of Central America, English or American.

Mr. Crowe, an English author, for many years a resident in the country, has drawn the characters of the opposing parties with an impartial hand. He says:

"The leaders of the Liberal party are composed of the élite of the Universities, many merchants and landed proprietors, supported by a numerous body, made up of the more intelligent artisans and laborers. * * * What they overthrew and accomplished for the State is honorable alike to their talents and sentiments; and though the limits of a sketch will scarcely admit of a due appreciation of it, a cursory view of their achievements will probably excite more wonder, and certainly secure for them higher praise, than the victories of Alvarado."

Of the Servile party, always the inexorable opponents of the Liberals, and now dominant in Guatemala and Costa Rica, he draws the following picture:

"The Serviles included the two extremes of society, linked together by their blind guides, the priests. Amongst them there were some few men of ability, although in this respect they were far inferior to the Liberals. * * * In general, if not universally, it will be found easy to trace to their intrigues the internal disorders of the social and political body in each of the States; and not a few of the past civil wars and existing animosities between the States are attributable to their influence, or to the personal ambition and seditious conduct of individuals in it."—*Crowe's Central America*, pp. 124, 126.

It was this Servile party which opposed the organization of the Republic of Central America, and sought to merge the country in the empire of Iturbide. Failing in this, they traitorously invited a force from Mexico, which, notwithstanding their armed concurrence, was defeated and destroyed by the Liberals. The same spirit now animates them, and the Government of Guatemala is seeking a similar union with the projected empire of Santa Anna. Its official paper for the last year has teemed with articles having this tendency, and denouncing and misrepresenting the United States, its institutions and policy. All the ribald abuse of the journals of Spain, Cuba, and Mexico is eagerly copied into its columns, and into those of its co-laborer, the official "Gazette of Costa Rica." Both are vehement in their advocacy of a union against the United States, whose policy is characterized as follows in an article published in the official paper of Guatemala, July 29, 1853:

"There is nevertheless one truth which the least informed cannot fail to recognize, because it is evident from all the events in the history of this continent, *viz.*, that the Anglo-Saxon race, which grows, multiplies, and strengthens daily in the North of America, is animated by a spirit of expansion and aggrandizement which tramples under foot all rules of international right. This spirit of aggression places in constant danger the Spanish race, which, in the midst of lamentable dissensions, is debilitated and consumed. Hence results the imperious necessity of the nations of this stock abandoning the chimeras which have deluded them and seeking, each one by itself and all together, to place a barrier against the unrestrained ambition which persecutes them."

Since the publication of the above, a more emphatic language has been adopted. In an article abusive of the present Attorney-General of the United States, the same paper prints the following paragraphs:

"Looking at the Inaugural Address of President Pierce, and to the remarks of Mr. Cushing, we deduce the dominant policy of the American Government to be one of *usurpation*, which should alarm not only the nations which surround the United States, but generally all civilized countries, who cannot see with indifference this modern Rome advance in a career of *aggression and rapine*," etc., etc., *ad nauseam*.

And still later, that is to say, in January last, the same paper, after a review of the events of the year, prognosticates a contest between the Americans and the Spanish stocks, "in which," it heroically adds, "Guatemala will not be found backward in defence of its race and religion"—in other words, it will fight the United States: a contingency from which we may well recoil in dismay!*

But the tendencies of the Governments of both Guatemala and Costa Rica may be inferred from the fact that the Secretary of State of the latter is a French refugee, lately Secretary to the notorious Flores in his attempts to *monarchize* the republics of South America; and that the most influential member of the Government of Guatemala is a Señor Pavon, former Private Secretary to the late equally notorious British Consul-General, Chatfield! *Par nobile fratrum!*

A cause may generally be judged by its leaders. Carrera, the Dictator of Guatemala, and Guardiola, expelled some years ago from Honduras for his crimes, are at the head of the war on Honduras. Who are these men? What is their history and character? These questions are amply answered by the following passages from the work of Mr. Dunlap on Central America. Mr. Dunlap, it may be observed, like Mr. Crowe, is an English author.

"Rafael Carrera, the Commander-in-Chief and President of the State of Guatemala, is a dark-colored and extremely ill-looking mestizo. He was originally servant to a woman of no very respectable character in Amatitlan, and afterwards

* "Notable events are no doubt destined to take place during the year 1854. A neighboring nation, (Mexico,) one of the most important of this continent, throwing resolutely aside the old prestiges of demagogical ideas, now seeks, with faith and without fear, the road which it should never have lost. Transcendental movements are preparing in that country which will necessarily effect great changes in the destiny of a considerable part of this continent.

"Meantime the influx of Americans, now in search of gold, and again to open routes between the seas, increases every day; and this very year may witness a general and decisive shock between the two rival races, of which the war with Mexico and the invasion of Cuba were only the precursors.

"In this combat, Guatemala has beforehand designated her place. Whenever they shall defend the Catholic faith; whenever they shall fight for the sentiment of race, there will float the flag of the young republic, which has been one of the first to proclaim the principles and sentiments which now appear to be recovering, every day more and more, their empire in the Spanish American States."—*Official Gazette of Guatemala, Jan. 6, 1854.*

to a Spaniard, from whom it is supposed he got the little knowledge and breeding he possessed when he first appeared on the political stage of Guatemala; afterwards, he was employed as a pig-driver; that is, in purchasing and personally driving pigs from the villages to Guatemala and the more populous towns.

"The Asiatic cholera having appeared in April, 1837, the Indians were led to believe that the waters had been poisoned by emissaries sent by the parties then ruling the state; and being also excited against the system of trial by jury, they united, to the number of some thousands, in the town of Santa Rosa, and under the command of Carrera, who had been one of the most active in deceiving them, destroyed a party of dragoons who had been sent out to disperse them. Carrera's faction was frequently defeated, and a vast slaughter made of the Indians who followed him at Villa Nueva, by the government troops under the command of Gen. Salazar, on the 11th Sept. 1838; but they have always reünited in greater force; and on the 13th of April, 1839, Carrera took Guatemala at the head of 5000 Indians; since which time he has retained all the real power in his hands. For some time he acted nominally under Mariano Rivera Paz, President of the State, but he has since dissolved the shadow of a representative assembly which existed; and having on the 19th of March, 1840, defeated Gen. Morazan, (the legal President of the republic,) by means of an immense superiority of force, and driven him out of Guatemala, after he had occupied it a day, he has since remained sole and supreme dictator of the State. * * * * * * By extortions and confiscations, he has amassed some hundreds of thousands of dollars in cash, lands, and houses; and it is consequently his interest to maintain a settled government and give protection to property; but in his private life he is more indecently immoral than could be conceived or understood by most English readers."

In respect to Guardiola, now next in command to Carrera, the same author observes:

"Guardiola is a dark-colored mestizo, stout-built, and rather corpulent, his face expressing his fiendish temper; but well liked by the soldiers, whom he indulges in every way. To his habits of intoxication may be added every species of vice which can be named among the vicious inhabitants of Central America; and frequently, in his drunken fits, he orders people to be shot who have in nothing offended him, while at all times the most trifling expression, incautiously uttered, is sufficient to cause the babbler to be shot without mercy. In private life he is as brutal as can well be imagined. In all the towns through which he passes, he makes a habit of calling in the best-looking women he can see, and, after subjecting them to infamous treatment, he drives them forth with the most insulting epithets; yet he is certainly the best and most successful general of any now existing, and, probably, of any who have appeared in Central America. Like Marius, the Roman leader, his brutal manners serve to terrify the enemy; hence, while the arrival of Cabañas and most of the other leaders is looked upon without fear by the people of the contending States, the bare mention of the name of Guardiola is sufficient to make the inhabitants fly to the woods, leaving every thing behind them."

In glorious contrast to these men stands Gen. Cabañas, the President of Honduras. As I have already said, during a long and active public life, he has never been guilty of an act which may not challenge the closest scrutiny. He was called the "right arm" of Gen. Morazan, the last President of Central America, in his struggles to maintain the Republic, and may dispute with him the honorable title of the ablest, purest, and most unselfish and truly patriotic man which Central America has ever produced. Mr. Stephens has borne emphatic testimony to his elevation of character and adherence to principle, and both Mr. Dunlap and Mr. Crowe refer to him in the same terms of praise, and as a contrast, in all respects, to the Indian Carrera, and the mestizo Guardiola!

I come now to the disreputable attack of your anonymous correspondent on the "Honduras Interoceanic Railway Company." As the venom of the scorpion lies in its tail, so the ill-concealed malice of your correspondent finds expression towards the close of his article, which seems to have been written to afford him an opportunity to relieve himself of a little troublesome personal spite. He comes to his point with the blunt inquiry, "Who are the projectors of the Honduras Railway Company?" And then, lacking manliness to make any direct charges against them, adopts the sneaking mode of propounding a series of questions, the design of which is to insinuate what he dares not aver.

In reply to your anonymous contributor's first question, it is proper to observe, it is none of his business, who are the projectors and beneficiaries of this Company. It is enough to say that it is composed of American citizens of the highest standing, some of whom have held eminent and responsible positions at home and abroad. Others rank high as merchants and men of enterprise, and all enjoy a well-earned reputation in society, upon which no anonymous scribbler, be he "retired citizen" or paid slanderer, can cast a blot. From their earliest relations with Honduras, springing out of the enterprise in which they are engaged, their efforts have been directed to preserve the public peace, and to establish harmony between Honduras and the other States. So far as their advice has been sought, or their influence exerted, both have been rendered in behalf of tranquillity. If they have not been successful in their efforts, it has been because the enemies of Honduras have refused all advances towards conciliation on the part of the latter, and because they are animated by a spirit of bitter hostility to her well-known liberal and American tendencies.

The Honduras Railroad Company are engaged in a laudable and legitimate enterprise, under a charter granted by the Government of Honduras, on principles of the widest liberality. If successful, they will throw open to the world a short and easy route between the seas, with unimpeachable harbors, and Free Ports at both extremities, and with a transit free to the citizens and products of all nations. In carrying out this enterprise, the Company have not, nor do they intend to stun the public ear with exaggerated statements, nor besiege the Government and Congress with schemes to further selfish ends. Nor do they employ "retired citizens" to misrepresent and slander other Companies engaged in similar enterprises. They are determined to carry out the task they have undertaken, without resort to any of the expedients which misdirected rivalry too often suggests, and which must always fail of their object.

Notwithstanding the exertions of the agents of the Honduras Co. in favor of peace in Central America, they have from the first been grossly abused by the organs and officers of Guatemala. But, unscrupulous as these proverbially are, they have never yet made the charges against the Company in which your correspondent indulges. Their opposition has been made on the direct ground that it is an *American* Company, and that it will confirm and solidify *American influence* in Honduras. Their opposition has been notoriously incited by the influence of all the European representatives in Guatemala, in precisely the same way that the hostility of Mexico was fanned into a flame, previous to the late war with that country. And it is a fact, susceptible of proof, that one particular reason why Guatemala rejects all overtures of peace from Honduras, and refuses the intervention of San Salvador and Nicaragua to that end, is the hope of interrupting the construction of the Road in question.

Under such circumstances, the Company will be justified, and it may consider itself called upon, to defend its rights from unwarrantable interference, by all means at its command.

Your correspondent is greatly exercised in consequence of an alleged exportation of arms to Honduras. That the Government of Honduras has purchased arms in the United States, which were regularly and publically shipped, is no doubt true. I am not aware that any attempt was ever made to disguise the fact. The transaction was a straightforward, commercial one, precisely like others which take place daily. The Honduras Railroad Company had sufficient faith in the honesty of Honduras to guarantee the payment of its purchases, and is prepared to do so, to any reasonable amount which that State may require. It is only to be hoped that the arms and ammunition purchased in New York, the produce of American labor, may prove superior to those which Guatemala has notoriously purchased in Belize, since the present difficulties commenced.

There is nothing in all this to call for the remonstrance which your correspondent asserts was made by that "Extraordinary Envoy" who bears upon his Atlantean shoulders the duties of Representative from all the undefined nooks and corners of creation, and whose inexhaustible titles crowd even the "ample verge" of the diplomatic pasteboard.* War has never been declared between Guatemala and Honduras, by either side; and the "outrages upon all the courtesies of international intercourse," which is alleged was committed by the parties in New York furnishing arms to Honduras, was no outrage at all, but a perfectly legitimate transaction, which may be repeated indefinitely without affording just grounds for censure from any quarter. No doubt Guatemala, having Belize close at hand, as a sort of dépôt, whence she may obtain her munitions of war, desires to prevent the other States from obtaining like supplies from other quarters. But I apprehend that she will have to adopt other means, to secure her monopoly of dangerous elements, than a hypocritical remonstrance to the American Secretary of State. The device is alike shallow and ludicrous; for no one can be deceived into considering Carrera's Indian forays (made without notice and without other authority than his own caprice, in true savage style) as wars, in any sense recognized amongst Christian nations.

Your anonymous correspondent undertakes to characterize the enterprise of the Honduras Railway Company as one "that has no intrinsic merits to recommend it." His competency to decide on that point may well be doubted, as he cannot possibly know any of the facts in the case. His impartiality may be judged by the spirit which he manifests. Having convicted him of misrepresentation and falsehood, and shown the malice which is concealed in every line of his communication, I leave him to the contempt and scorn of all men who respect honor and regard truth.

In conclusion, I can only express my surprise and regret, that the "Intelligencer" has permitted itself to become the medium for the gratification of personal spite, and the dissemination of falsehoods such as crowd the communication of its anonymous correspondent.

I am, respectfully,

Your obedient servant,

E. Geo. SQUIER.

New-York, March 20, 1854.

---

* Reference is here made to Don Felipe Molina, "Envoy Extraordinary and Minister Plenipotentiary from Guatemala, Costa Rica, and San Salvador." The "retired citizen" of the *Intelligencer* is supposed to be a certain Mr. Kerr, who was a year or two in Nicaragua as U. S. Chargé d'Affaires, where he distinguished himself by——drawing his salary! History has failed to record his other achievements.

www.ingramcontent.com/pod-product-compliance
Lightning Source LLC
LaVergne TN
LVHW010832120826
845149LV00016B/1295

* 9 7 8 1 4 1 8 1 9 0 3 8 5 *